Living in a Desert

Patty Whitehouse

Rourke

Publishing LLC

Vero Beach, Florida 32964

www.rourkepublishing.com

PHOTO CREDITS: © Lynn M. Stone: pages 15, 16, 17; © Steven Alan: page 4; © Ulrike Haimmerich: page 7; © Cheryrl A. Meyer: page 7; © Michael Westhoff: page 9; © Jose Carlos Pires pereira: page 9; © Janine White: page 11; © Steve Faupel: page 12; © Kevdog 818: page 14; © Jill Fromer: page 19; © Peter Adams: page 20; © Vera Gobaerts: page 21; © Jason Cheever: page 22; © Grifin Hammond: page 22; © Seraphicole: page 13.

Editor: Robert Stengard-Olliges

Cover and interior design by Nicola Stratford

Library of Congress Cataloging-in-Publication Data

Whitehouse, Patricia, 1958-
  Living in a desert / Patty Whitehouse.
       p. cm. -- (Animal habitats)
  Includes index.
  ISBN 1-60044-183-1 (hard cover)
  ISBN 1-59515-543-0 (soft cover)
  1. Deserts--Juvenile literature. I. Title. II. Series: Whitehouse, Patricia, 1958- Animal habitats.

  QH88.W48 2007
  578.754--dc22

                                        2006017658

Printed in the USA

CG/CG

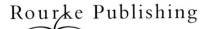

Rourke Publishing

www.rourkepublishing.com – sales@rourkepublishing.com
Post Office Box 3328, Vero Beach, FL 32964

TABLE OF CONTENTS

WHAT IS A DESERT?

Deserts are dry places. Deserts do not get a lot of rain.

Some deserts are hot in the day and cold at night.

HOW ARE DESERT PLANTS DIFFERENT?

Some plant parts are thick and fat. They store water for the plant.

Some plants grow only when it rains. Some plants have small leaves. Some have spines.

SPINES AND LEAVES

Cactus plants have thick stems and **spines**. The tallest cactus is the saguaro.

Mesquite is a **shrub** with tiny leaves. It has a long, long **root**.

FLOWERS

Some desert plants do not grow all year. They grow flowers only after it rains.

This desert plant looks like a rock most of the time.

After it rains, a flower grows from its leaves.

HOW ARE DESERT ANIMALS DIFFERENT?

Some desert animals sleep when it is hot. Others live under the ground.

Desert animals cannot find much water. Some get water from the food they eat.

STINGERS AND BEAKS

Scorpions are awake at night in the desert. They use their stinger and pinchers to catch food.

Many birds live in the desert. Owls and wrens make **nests** in cactus plants.

SCALY ANIMALS

The thorny devil is a desert lizard. It only eats ants.
It drinks water that falls on its back.

The sidewinder is a snake. It moves sideways on the desert sand.

BiG HUMPS AND EARS

Camel humps are made of fat. Camels can go without food or water for two weeks.

Jack rabbits have big ears. Their ears help them keep cool.

Some desert animals find shade and water in an oasis.

Without these green and wet places. Some animals could not survive living in the desert.

CAN PEOPLE LIVE IN DESERTS?

People have lived in deserts for a long time. They found ways to keep cool and find water.

Glossary

nest (NEST) — place where birds lay their eggs

shrub (SHRUB) — plant smaller than a tree

spines (SPINEZ) — leaves that look like needles

root (ROOT) — part of a plant that grows under the ground

Index

FURTHER READING

Jackson, Kay. *Deserts.* Bridgestone Books, 2006.

Legg, Gerald. *Life in the Desert.* Children's Press, 2005.

Whitehouse, Patricia. *Hiding in the Desert.* Heinemann Library, 2004.

WEBSITES TO VISIT

www.mbgnet.net

www.enchantedlearning.com/coloring/oceanlife.shtml

www.desertusa.com/life.html

ABOUT THE AUTHOR

Patty Whitehouse has been a teacher for 17 years. She is currently a Lead Science teacher in Chicago, where she lives with her husband and two teenage children. She is the author of more than 100 books about science for children.